KT-466-249

BEGINNING HISTORY

THE GUNPOWDER PLOT

Rhoda Nottridge

Illustrated by Mark Stacey

TROUBLED TIMES

Over 400 years ago, **Catholics** and **Protestants** in Britain argued fiercely about their different religious **beliefs**.

Catholic churches were forced to give their valuables to Henry VIII.

Catholics were people who thought that the **Pope** in Rome should be the head of the English Church. But King **Henry VIII** had **declared** that he, not the Pope, was the head of the English Church. People who agreed with the King were called Protestants.

5

THE CATHOLICS SUFFER

By the time **James I** became King, Catholics had suffered terrible punishments at the hands of their **rivals**. James I was a Protestant and he treated the Catholics harshly.

Catholic **priests** were hunted out and sometimes killed. People known to be Catholics were punished for their beliefs.

It was during these hard times that a Catholic man called Guy Fawkes returned to England from abroad.

Above *This is an old portrait of King James I of England and VI of Scotland.*

Right *During this period both Catholics and Protestants would treat each other unfairly when they were in power. This is a drawing of Protestants destroying a Catholic church.*

Guy Fawkes seeing
the arrest of a
Catholic priest.

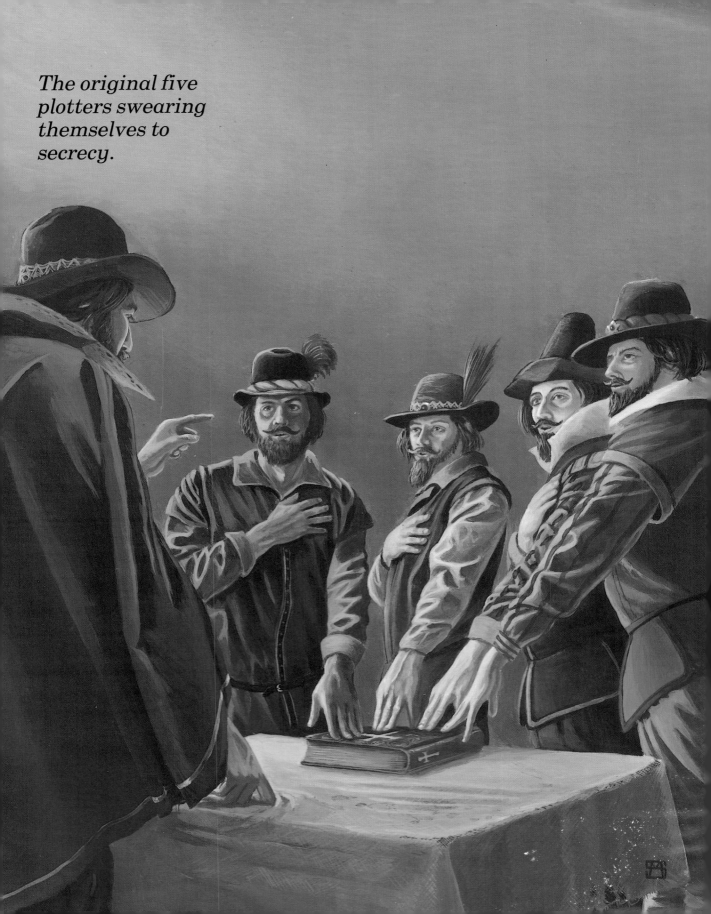

The original five plotters swearing themselves to secrecy.

A SECRET MEETING

Guy Fawkes had been asked to come back to England by a man called Robert Catesby. Fawkes went to Catesby's house to find out why he wanted him.

At Catesby's house, Guy Fawkes met two of his old schoolfriends, Thomas Percy and John Wright, and another man, Thomas Winter. They were all Catholics. Catesby made all the men swear an **oath** of secrecy. Then he told them about his plot.

Above *Guy Fawkes.*

Below *The plotters, from a pamphlet of the time.*

THE PLOT BEGINS

Catesby believed that the only way to get rid of the harsh King and his **Parliament** was to blow them all up with gunpowder!

Top *The modern Houses of Parliament, London.*

Above *King James I and his Parliament.*

Opposite *The plotters begin the tunnel.*

The other men agreed. They **rented** a house next to the Parliament buildings. The plot was to dig a tunnel through to the cellars of the Parliament buildings. Then, they would fill the cellars with gunpowder. On the day Parliament opened, with the King present, they would blow the whole lot up.

HARD WORK

Digging the tunnel was not going to
be easy. The walls of the Parliament
buildings' cellars were nearly 3 m
thick! The men carried on digging,
hidden underneath the rented house.

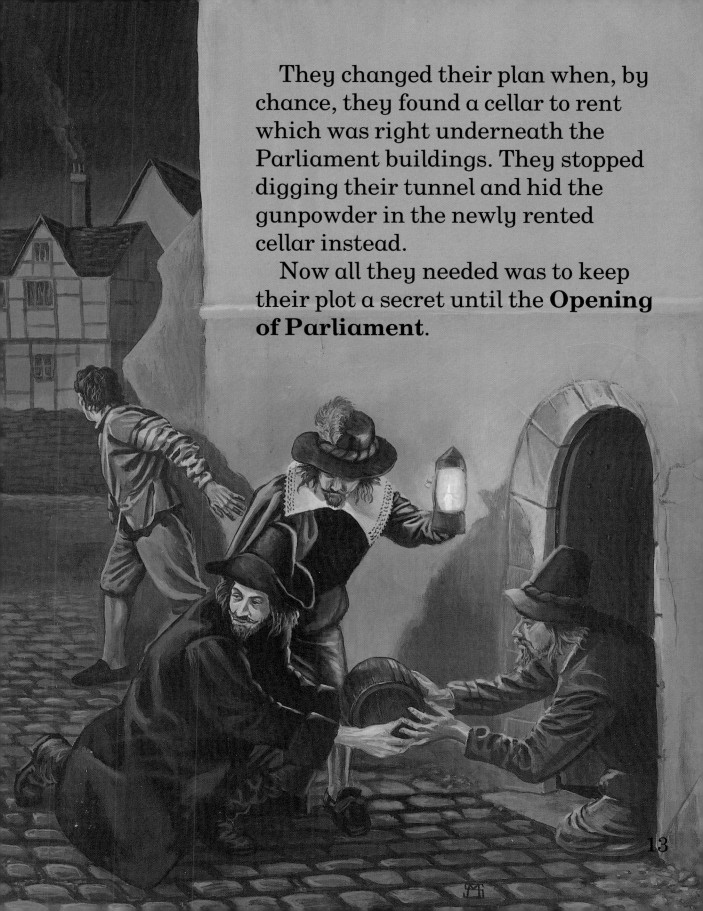

They changed their plan when, by chance, they found a cellar to rent which was right underneath the Parliament buildings. They stopped digging their tunnel and hid the gunpowder in the newly rented cellar instead.

Now all they needed was to keep their plot a secret until the **Opening of Parliament**.

13

THE PLOT THICKENS

The plotters were running out of enough money to stay in hiding. To raise more, they decided to tell some rich Catholics about their plot.

Francis Tresham was the thirteenth man to join the 'gunpowder plot'. Guy Fawkes did not trust Tresham with their secret. He was right to worry.

Top *A cartoon of the time showing God watching the plotters' movements.*

Above *A later illustration of all thirteen plotters.*

Opposite *Tresham being told of the plot.*

Tresham realized that his brothers-in-law would be at the Opening of Parliament. He panicked, in case they would be blown up.

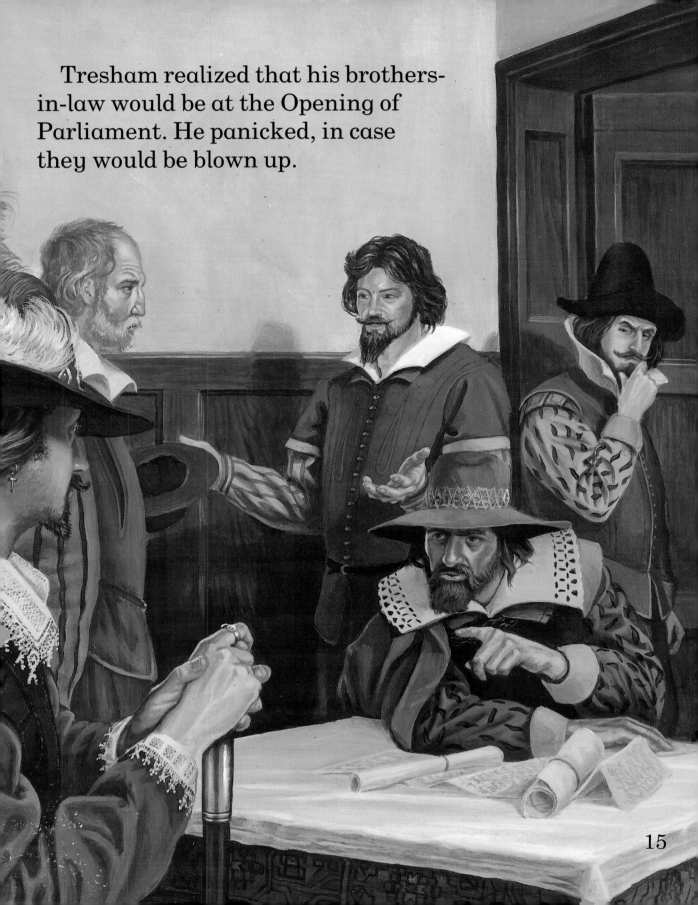

*Lord Monteagle
hurrying to warn
King James and the
Parliament of danger.*

16

A WARNING

Tresham begged the other plotters to stop the plan. Catesby promised that, two days before the Opening of Parliament, he would find a secret way of warning Tresham's brothers-in-law not to go to the **ceremony**.

Ten days before Catesby's warning was due, someone sent Lord Monteagle, one of Tresham's brothers-in-law, an **anonymous letter**. It warned him of the 'gunpowder plot'. Monteagle got on his horse and galloped off to show the letter to the King.

An illustration of the scene of Lord Monteagle having received the warning letter.

DISCOVERED!

On the night of 4 November 1605, Guy
Fawkes waited in the rented house
next to the Parliament buildings. In
just a few hours, he would go round to
the cellars and light the **fuse** to the

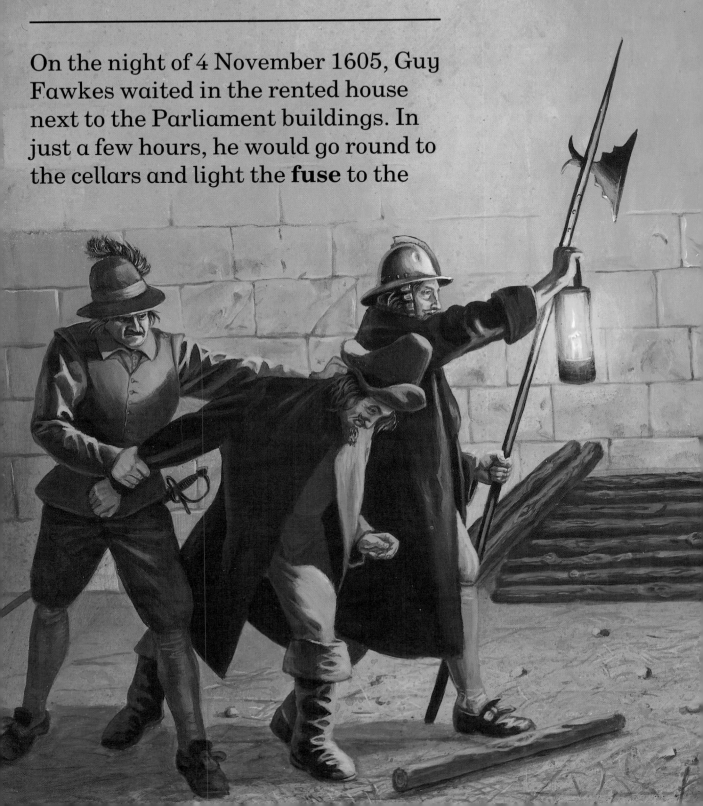

gunpowder. The King and Parliament would be blown to pieces!

It was not to be. Because of Monteagle's warning the King's soldiers found Guy Fawkes, with matches and a fuse hidden in his clothing. The gunpowder in the cellar was also discovered.

Guy Fawkes being arrested in the Parliament buildings' cellars.

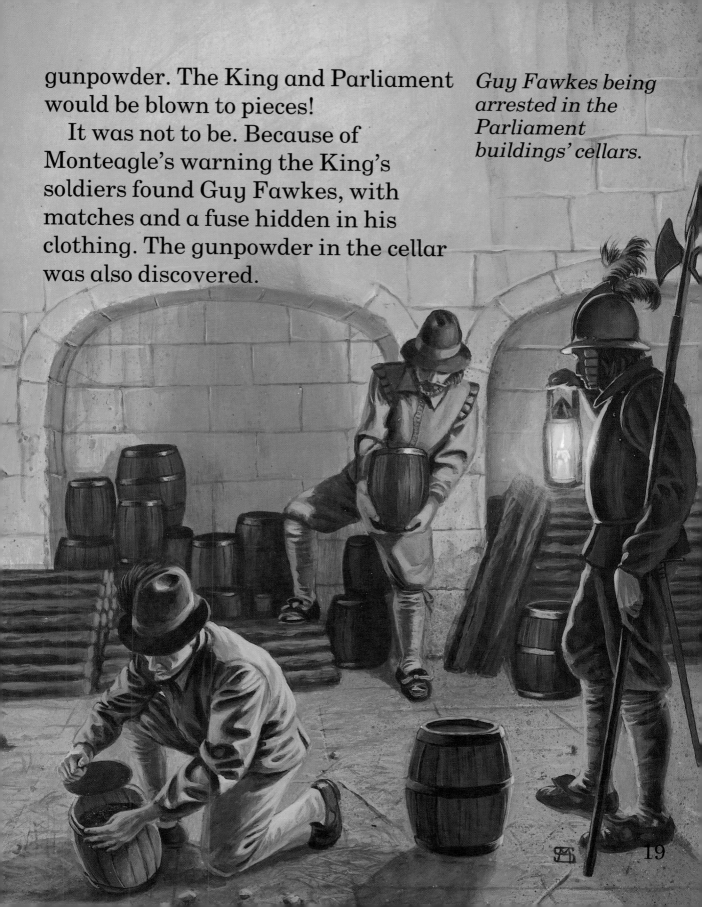

REMEMBER, REMEMBER . . .

Guy Fawkes and the other plotters were either executed or died while trying to escape the King's soldiers.

On the night of 5 November 1605, people **loyal** to the King celebrated

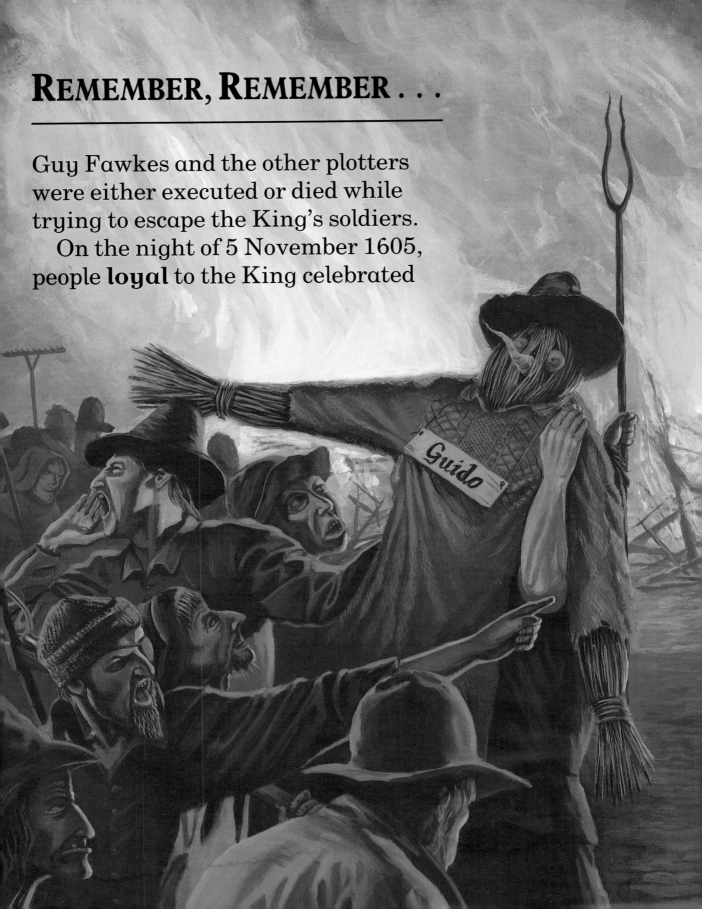

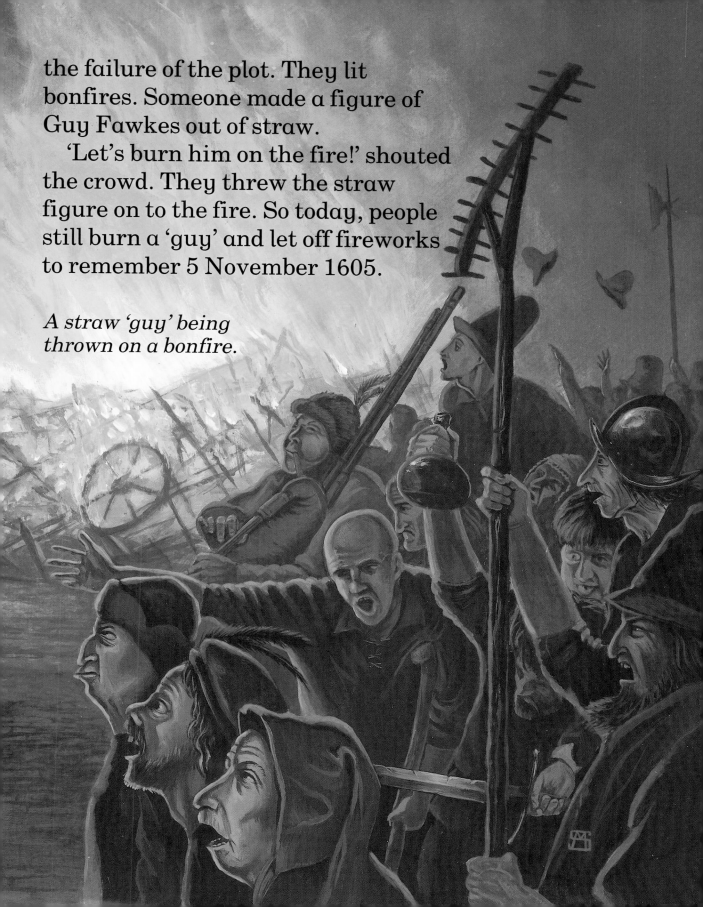

the failure of the plot. They lit bonfires. Someone made a figure of Guy Fawkes out of straw.

'Let's burn him on the fire!' shouted the crowd. They threw the straw figure on to the fire. So today, people still burn a 'guy' and let off fireworks to remember 5 November 1605.

A straw 'guy' being thrown on a bonfire.

GLOSSARY

Anonymous letter A letter that is not signed by the person who wrote it.

Beliefs The ideas that people think are right.

Catholics Christians who believe that the leader of their church is the Pope in Rome, Italy.

Ceremony A special way of marking an important occasion.

Declared Made a statement which said something quite definitely.

Fuse A long lead which is lit and burns slowly. When it reaches gunpowder, a lit fuse makes the gunpowder explode.

Henry VIII King of England from 1509 to 1547.

James I King of England from 1603 to 1625. He had already been King of Scotland since 1567.

Loyal To be faithful and trusting.

Oath A very serious promise.

Opening of Parliament The ceremony when the King or Queen, Lords and Members of Parliament meet to start work again after a long break.

Parliament The group of people who represent the citizens of Britain when laws and rules are being passed. There are two groups, the House of Commons and the House of Lords and they meet in the Palace of Westminster in London.

Pope The head of the Catholic Church who lives in Rome, Italy.

Priests People authorized to conduct religious services.

Protestants Christians who do not belong to the Catholic Church.

Rented Paid money to use a house or building belonging to someone else.

Rivals People who compete against each other for a similar goal or motive.

BOOKS TO READ

Crown and Parliament by R J Unstead (A & C Black 1979)

Growing Up in Stuart Times by Madeline Jones (Batsford 1979)

Gunpowder, Treason and Plot by Lewis Winstock (Wayland Publishers 1987)

Henry VIII by Dorothy Turner (Wayland Publishers 1988)

It's Fun Finding Out About Long Ago by Deborah Manley (Kingfisher 1988)

Kings and Queens of England by L Du Garde Peach (Ladybird 1981)

Picture acknowledgements

The publishers would like to thank the following for providing the photographs in this book: Bridgeman Art Library 6 (both); The Mansell Collection 10 (bottom), 14; Mary Evans Picture Library 9 (top); Syndication International 10 (top); Topham Picture Library 9 (bottom); Wayland Picture Library 14 (top), 17.

INDEX